MW01142863

SHAMELESS

SHAMELESS

MARLENE COOKSHAW

Brick Books

National Library of Canada Cataloguing in Publication Data

Cookshaw, Marlene–
    Shameless

Poems.
ISBN 1-894078-21-7

    I. Title

PS8555.O573S53 2002   C811'.54   C2001-904093-8
PR9199.3.C6416S53 2002

We gratefully acknowledge the Canada Council for the Arts, the
Government of Canada through the Book Publishing Industry
Development Program (BPIDP), and the Ontario Arts Council
for their support of our publishing programme.

The cover image is from 'Blue Hare', a screen print by Sophie
Ryder.
The author's photo is by Mitchell Parry.

This book is set in Gill Sans and Perpetua.

Design and layout by Alan Siu.

Printed and bound by Sunville Printco Inc.

Brick Books
431 Boler Road, Box 20081
London, Ontario   N6K 4G6

brick.books@sympatico.ca

for my sisters

Contents

"The tiny silver luck of minnows"

A man and his daughter drift
in an open boat on St Mary's Lake.

He fishes, she reads, almost without
lifting her head, a shabby red-

bound book unearthed from the basement
called *A Friend of Caesar*. Nothing to do

with Rome or even friendship; I can't
recall what happens. The other

summer novels: Jack London,
Mountains of the Moon—not

science fiction. Fooled again. The lake
is as blue as could be imagined, the sky

chicory blossom gone milky
with cloud. No one catches fish.

Her father seems happy to sit with her
there, he with his thoughts

and she with her book, but I see now
from thirty years this side of that

dammed lake, man-made, he doesn't like
the fixity of her attention on the book.

"Look out for the hook," is what
he would say, were not words themselves

the fragments of fear, a school of fear
rising, shimmering, aching to breach

that temperate, impenetrable blue.

Genesis Again

New rain hammers the sunbaked shingles
on the attic roof over the bath:

determined and dreadful, like the dog's nails
grappling two flights of stairs, like a creature

newly wakened and lonely and looking for me:
Are you there? Are you there? Ah,

you're here—I've been sleeping, under the blue
Italian blanket twitched aside. The sun

went in; my grey brow sparked and fizzed and,
when my heart dropped, minerals scattered

throughout the clawfoot pond you put a foot in,
bath bomb unsettling its porcelain shallows.

Having realized you here, I heave a deep
dog's sigh. You submerge. I lay myself down.

Davis Road

Twice this week, late morning,
the young Rottweiler has announced

my passing. Those walks were sunlit,
the greetings clipped and gruff. Today

it's wet; he moans; his fogged report is
muted, without hope. By walking past

I've stirred him merely to awareness
of the drizzle, his place in a wet yard,

tethered and young, the spark of his being
rained to ash. In the distance

a terrier questions what it hears.
But the Rottweiler's low soft-pedalled howl's

unmodified by bitterness and can conceive
no ear. Nor I, until a hummingbird plunges

electric through the pines. So perfectly
does it pierce the dog's lament

and label it that I speed up to put behind me
such despair—which is the dwelling

of each animal that's thrown its lot in with us.
And of our children as time in increments

reveals the mineshaft of our hearts. We are
desolate ourselves and cannot save them.

Rain and more rain. Eloquent, it loosens
the possible. A little,
                    then more, you see

how it lets itself down.

Kouros

You are standing here though you are gone
a thousand miles:

The green world shines, an apple deep
under ice
                    —John Thompson, "The Great Bear"

The ice may fail at any step,
and does: two Dene men fall through

and Billy dies. The unnamed one survives.
He tells the story as an odyssey,

a lifetime. Describes disorder
before I know the medium.

When I turn on the radio
he is already under ice.

The voice without a name survives.
His father drowned in 1971

and he was then fifteen, so he's
about my age and also fatherless.

Oh, there was snow where I grew up,
and ice, and treachery, but salted well

and gravelled to a measure
of stability. For the blind, it's said,

there is no roof until it thunders.
For him, engulfed, roof is the only

solid: he's suspended in what
time might be if it were nearly

visible and thickened in the cold.
Under the ice he thrashes, his terror

bottomless, ballooning with his clothes
until, lucid for a moment, he recalls

his father died while in the water too,
and this is comfort, this brings calm.

He can in fact inhale his father: woodsmoke,
canvas, sweat embrace him, lay him on his back.

I listen to this story in a basement,
dressed for bed. The window's closed

against an August weekend's noise,
shade drawn. He calls it dim

before I know the element. He says
it is not dark as night,

but hazy, indistinct. I stop wandering
and sit. He is exactly right.

His father's smell returns to him
entire: a blanket they shared once

in winter camp. The blanket then
was vast above them, knit,

but under ice it is an infant's sling;
he lets his tired arms drift.

Imagine underwater skyed
by ice that cracks with any weight.

I hesitate beside the bed, and sink,
hairbrush in my lap. Attentive,

keen, the ice, despotic as the bathroom glass.
The voice beneath it deepens, slows.

By 1986 I'd long forgot my father's smell.
That year it was disclosed he lived a life

before us. All men do, of course,
but most men live their lives in order,

and before they die. My father, buried
then for thirteen years, got up and married,

bore two sons and dug a grave for one,
divorced, and left the church.

He'd never seen that hairbrush
in my hand, or knew what I'd become,

and the man I thought I'd loved
I'd never known. The nameless

one survives. Suspended in the arms
of his drowned father, he remembers

how it was, and how his mother cried.
His brothers, sisters. Then it grips him

at the core: he is a man himself, with wife
and children: horrified at what

he knows—no, *undergoes*, it bites—
they are, they will be subject to his death.

So he decides he will not die.

In this abyss, green, cloudy–no, those words
are mine. He says, Not as dark as night.

He says he sees, a little, round him.

Below him in the water, then, a man, who
sinks, whose arms trail overhead. Billy?

Not Billy. Not another's arms at all,
they are his own, this man is him; and

shocked, he tries to get back in, to move
those limbs. On the second try it works,

he pushes, agonized, against
his sodden clothing and the loss

of that cradle of his father's smell. He hauls
himself, embodied, onto ice.

He heaves himself onto the ice; it breaks.

It is thirty degrees below zero. He goes
under for more than a minute.

He loses the opening.

This time, rising, he nudges Billy
going down. Here's Billy's face, his eyes.

He watches. Billy dies. He finds
another opening. This one's rimmed

with thicker ice, less brittle.
His hands are in the air. And then he's out.

I listen to this in a basement
dressed for bed. I lose the opening.

Two Dene men slip through,
and Billy dies. Dispirited, his body

plunges like carved stone. *Kouros.*
What would hold us now streams overhead.

He tells a story. I prepare for bed.
All this time I hold a hairbrush in my hand,

empty of all except Billy and him,
who is still nameless, who lives, tells

the tale as though it were a history,
a voyage charted to its own course under

water dense with shades. His mother,
siblings; his own wife and children;

his dead friend, his father's smell. Under ice
an ether, vast and green, where canvas

slid an arm beneath his back,
woodsmoke cupped a hand beneath his head.

Into the dark smell of his father
his wife and children dropped a brighter hook.

Room 418

I'm lying on my back as light
falls away from the sky, which all day

has burned raw and substantial; now dark
slides a mask between me and the face

of the mountain defining my view. Things
arrive at their end. A man and a woman

walk the long hall, anticipate night.
My companion's recorder holds a high

note. On the newly made bed on my back I
read Philip Levine: *What Work Is*.

The woman who saunters the hall
with legs like a girl's wears wool the deep blue

of a winter night sky embroidered with glittering
glass. *What Work Is*: a library book

overdue, a book I won't finish. I read
each poem slowly and some of them twice.

The recorder punctuates the falling
dark like birdsong; lamp and pillows

—and look, now my face—develop
the place the mountain was.

Outdoor Baptism

after a photo by Thurston Hatcher

That the *Saturday Evening Post*
of 1958 could unfold such
a heart: a two-page spread,
a lake like milk, and into it
a row of posts the eye can ride
to heaven.
        How to live one's life
in a calm that glacial?

To the right the noisy neighbourhood
has gathered in its multicoloured best
beneath the pines, and sprawls
among the dark columnar trunks
like flowers of one vine:
hyacinth bean or cup-and-saucer
tethering the shore.
        The girl's
in water to her waist.
Bare-armed. Her hands are clasped
within the grip of Pastor Blackwell

whose right arm reaches high
to haul the holy spirit down.
When he has it in his fist, he'll
slap it to her neck and tip
her backward.
        Baptism:
           that
moment when shame flees and we're made
pure, a burning underwater, an unlocking
of the skull.
        Her white shirt

opened to the sternum, she'll drop
beneath the surface of this life, then rise up

streaming, newborn, sleek,
radiant.

And this, I think, is also true:

A part of her will never rise,
will bottom-feed Lake Grandview, its water
muddied by the sinners' clumsy feet.

A part sheers off and lights
the Sharptop peak.
                    The body's left,
the bruised and brilliant
flesh: her nipples rise to August air,
her thighs are slicked to the wet skirt.

The women, hatted, pursed, will rush
to cover her with towels. She'd rather

roll her body dry on duff
and roots. Her soul's a flight path
to the ring of Blue Ridge Mountains.
She's married something,
                              something
has broken her; the bees
explore her dripping arms, which swim
ashore to half of Jasper, Georgia, gathered
on the second Sunday of the month to witness
what the faithless cannot fathom. I want to say,

Let go what you don't want
to her bowed head. Keep moving.
The river of your spirit has a current
stronger than you know. Let

go. Keep going. Be
shameless.

One Wave

If all's perception anyway, why not perceive
what makes us happy? If it does no harm,

I tell myself, if nothing's missed: We must
be vigilant. Well-dressed, inveterate.

The dunes are pierced, miraculously,
with peavine, eelgrass, strawberries and broom.

They rise from sand—which has no repeatable shape
but is sucked by our boots and tossed

in a spray down the beach. Habit: what we
put on. The clothing of our spirits. Times

when all I wanted was the next to be
familiar. Horizon. Night sky. Lover. Food.

What washes up are milky muscles of the sea,
paling to moonstone and barred with purple.

How I travel by map, how I cross
the dunes to the wild beach and look back

at the numbered pillars. One wave
ripples and races, all froth and circumstance,

ringed curtain released
by an impatient nurse. Loss is loss:

the death to us of someone, too like
the death of someone. Not the same,

but too like. We keep what we can.
Home is gesture, repeated.

Elbow on Knee

Before all voyages by car, on the eve
of my sister's wedding, Good Fridays also,

my father prays with his family.
By the footstool of my mother's chair

he plucks his trouser crease
between fingers that know best machines,

and know them intimately, the way their souls
can be eased with gravity and grease,

and drops to one knee, seizing
the gaze of his daughters, who

can neither look nor look away. He drops
to one knee, his left, gives up

the trappings of this world.
His right hand cups his forehead.

I don't know what I am to do. My mother
has swept the hall and scrubbed the sink. Suitcases

are lined up by the car. If this
is Friday, it will be long, and what's ahead

unknowable. If my sister's getting married,
the fifty covered buttons of her gown are

perfect. Elbow on knee, that is how he prays,
drawing all light in the room

to the palm of his hand. When
he lowers his head, night falls.

Planetesimal

Farthest planet, Pluto, from the heart, though
not always, its orbit severely

elliptic, estrangement from the sun
sometimes thirty, sometimes fifty that of Earth's.

All cycles are delicate, of course, all threaten
to cease repeating, to swing

into an orbit so far from circular
nothing can be counted on. These things

happen. Like snow. The chickens hate it,
the snow, which lights up the night.

The rooster screams, the pullet
looks confused, the hen determined.

Pluto is barely two-thirds of our moon,
and winter's 124 years long. Uncharted

when my parents were young,
the universe was smaller, less detailed.

What can numbers teach us anyway? Proportion,
a little. Eventually. Pluto has

its own moon, revealed only
the year I left the glacier-scraped prairie

with my dog, for the green place
where mountains reared up from the sea.

Charon is half the size of Pluto. They
are really twin planets, rock and ice,

planetesimals, adolescent, unfinished
as Earth when flung out from the sun.

Unwanted and eloquent as snow in late spring.
It falls again in this season, soft and heavy

as a child's eyelids, as memory, as down
the hen herself has plucked to line the nest.

Bruise

Looking backward
we back into
life. Its finest particle
surprises. Through

the rear window of cars
in the years before seatbelts, or
standing on ship stern:
exquisite, unbearable arc

of each detail surging
away. Back
as shield, carapace
of bone and muscle, what splits

the world in two
—the right, the left—
and serves it up
in passing. What passes

for highway, landscape, ship's
wake, its populace of gulls.
I'm not certain I'm ready
to turn, or ever will be: someone

needs to note the extravagant
waste of our lives, its drop-dead
beauty. Like that splay
of prairie landfill I hand-fed

with remnants of
my mother's basement. Broken
TVs, calendars
across the heaps of glittering

trash—which bulldozers fold,

relentless, into earth, like laundry,
while in the distance sun picks out
the reds of lampshades, aprons.

The gulls lift off and land
with every turn of the machines.
This happens north of a town
whose only honoured road

runs east and west.
South is America, north
the frontier. Always
I've packed and gone west,

over mountains, my back
to the town I grew up in,
to the wavering path my father traced
in this world, then abandoned.

Did he look backward
too? There we are standing back
to back: a strong position, good
defence, the last defence.

An embrace of a kind.
In its way.

The Thumbprint of the Picker

1

Deep in the bush and not so long ago
Elizabeth heard from her dying father's lips
the news that she had a sister, half-sister,
whom she sought out and grew to love dearly.

Winifred was three years her senior, also
lonely, also pear-shaped, also blonde.
Imagine them together, two golden fruit
on the far edge of ripeness, laughing gently, one

with a father who went to buy cigarettes
when she was two and returned when she was eight,
the other with a father she remembered only
hazily with her mother, drinking and smoking.

How they burned for each other, she recalled,
how they burned each other out. The blonde sisters
live with a canary named Brie, creamy yellow
and sharp-voiced. They themselves are serene,

turning memories in their laps, sipping
white wine at an open air cafe on the lake
in the afternoon before the bugs come out.

2

Fruit flies have been genetically altered
to sing on the eighteenth hour of their day
and then die young. Or they can be left to live
eight hours more and sing at six o'clock.

In a glass bowl pears will ripen evenly,
perfect. Though always a spot
will appear, the thumbprint of the picker.
Each man collects in time a modest pyramid

of women: mother, sisters, lovers, daughters. All
if consumed in the right order will prove exactly
ripe and satisfying and leave him wanting more.
Like code inscribed in lemon juice, the print:

what's been impressed emerges, rots us
unless we're eaten soon. Are women meant
then to be eaten? Who means us?
This continues to

confound me. But I know this: men will
consume us. They mean that we should ripen, full
of juice, just so, and never show a bruise.

Letter to a Husband Who's Moved Out

The kettle spits on the woodstove, into which
I have just stuffed the ragged bits of these hard months.

And though they spill out, burning, onto the hearth tile,
I control them with the shovel and horsehair brush,

keep them from rising too high on their own hot breath.
The sun climbs the ridge behind me, having taken

a long time to reach the west coast of America
and dragging with it the tawny heat of desert stone.

The spade-shaped balsam leaves unearth
a fierce, remedial perfume: essential oil

of deep rock split by sun. Drunk on it,
I tell you this, in faith and out of love:

when the rank water has receded into mud
and ducks mope under evergreens, I will have

taken sun into the seedcoat of my heart and started
something I can't see, and fear the end of. Stars

will have swivelled in the Lazy Susan sky.

Snakes on all the paths lie certain
of their speed. The herbs and grey-leaved santolina

bask, and thistles surge to meet
the dipping goldfinch. Wild grass

in the wet field will wave above my head
and muzzle the cicadas' chronic buzz.

I'll walk past the rotting alder over which
the Guernsey Cream clematis blooms, and sit

beside the pond. The questing mouths of goldfish
pock its calm like ghosts of rain.

In the thicket this overheated season has become,
wrens and finches stitch the air between the ripening

berries, the towhees rage; the hummingbirds work
their own vertical tapestry in the clearing

you hacked out between the hawthorne and the hedge.

Chatelaine

In the middle of the empty room my sister sits
on a straight-backed chair, an enormous

rag doll on her lap. She has just embroidered
its features, realistic, uncommonly

sweet, despite her use of pink for eyes
as well as nose. The long legs drape across her own

while she stuffs them. With what, I ask, because
they are weighty and dense. Oh, she says, various

things, she knew she'd find odds and ends here,
and did, she nods at the hat shelf inside the front door.

The doll is a Christmas gift for my mother, and I think,
How generous, The time it took, and also, What an odd gift, almost

lifesize. Look here, my sister says, turning
its back. The doll wears hair in greyish profusion,

about to be rolled—as my mother's is—in a silver sausage
like those Renaissance silk crowns in astonishing colours,

then pinned to the back of her head.

Nice Girls

don't sit like that.
She says. We are

to keep our knees together,
ask no energy from earth.

We are to circle it:
small planets, moons

in aprons. So. Legs angled
obliquely, we

orbit. A mother denies her daughters
a firm grip on the earth.

Satellites. Withdrawn. Unstable.
The gravity of this eludes her.

When the Light Changed

My dog was always, until
he grew deaf in old age, afraid
of thunder, gunshot, anything that cracked. Also
the noise the shades made upon rising.

At first we weren't sure if he
liked this or hated it; at the beginning
we'd pull, a sharp tug, he'd come running,
bark and appear deeply interested.

We raised and lowered the shade a few times
for his entertainment.
                        But on the sixth day
he dredged a sound so Permian we smelled
the peat bogs flare. Under the spell of it

sequoias toppled; dragonflies starred
the bloody dust. I was carried by the back of the neck
in my mother's teeth, watched
belugas give birth to their young, premature.

He gave voice to the seasons out of order.
Flies constellated the south window. Crows
took a stand in the cottonwood. Many
small goldfish rose to the bait.

With scarcely a pause that howl
unwound. We were washed by black tea
to the finest wire of thought:
                        how could we?
How could we ever have believed this to be play?

A breath more resonant than his or ours had called
attention to itself. From then on one of us
would rub his ears in the back room when
the light changed. Trucks could pass, or children

with their guns. Flushed from cover
morning and evening the soul more dimly fluttered
from someone else's quick, efficient hands.

The Field

morning by singular morning,
and shell by broken shell
—Mary Oliver, "Morning Walk"

I slept three hours in the hospital chair last night,
another two this afternoon in bed. And so can stumble
through the rutted field that flanks my sister's yard,
trailing my husband, who walks the family dog.

My mother's forgotten her week-old decision to die.
I think it was this she looked for last night: the missing
tooth, ideal arrangement of the limbs.
Today her body takes again the path begun.

The field speaks endlessly of loss: the bleak sun gone
behind a cloud provokes the evening cries of birds:
sweet, aspiring, brief. How is it possible to hold
death like a stone in our heads while the earth sings?

The cornstubble field, abandoned, is on its way to lots.
Smaller each season. Next year it will be gone
to hydro wires, sidewalks, and equidistant ornamental
trees younger than we are, and so not possibly more wise.

My mother's childlike sweetness amazed us half a day.
Not long: death won't keep company with time.
Closer to death yesterday than days before. Ungraspable
proximity. It subdivides. And, closer still, today.

Figure and Ground

On the crest of the Astoria Bridge, about to
swing the long dip into Washington State,

what's ahead is a wholeness of water
sundered by wet road: impossible to unplait

as that trick with figure and ground
that asks you to choose face or vase.

The water's a grey field, what feeds us;
the road through reaped and tamped

by tractors, bare feet, July sun. But
all here is grey: blue-grey or grey-grey.

On Washington waves bob two dozen
geese, up and down, up and down,

vanishing by degrees along the coast. Music
says what it says complete, accordion-folded:

there's a trick, it is possible to cut
an opening large enough to step through

in a musical score just six inches square. So
I do. A figure on ground, I drive

the bridge that does not arc but dips,
and climb the far bank behind an empty

cattle truck that tosses spray and billows
roadside brush like pegged green laundry.

In the rearview a pair of nuclear reactors
flicker; their turrets wear tiaras in the mist; ahead

six cars in a meadow with headlights on
halo a burning barn. That counterpoint

colours the Jerseys, alfalfa, sequoia,
the speed at which we travel. Between

Blue Slough Road and Montesano, the red open mouths
at the end of their drives await the *Daily World*.

Niagara

A thousand mushrooms crowd to a keyhole.
This is the one star in their firmament
Or frames a star within a star.
What should they do there but desire?
        —Derek Mahon, "A Disused Shed in County Wexford"

The cells of my mother's body turn from light,
directed by her will, uncommon, queenly. She
orders her affairs, convokes her daughters,
one by one, long distance, to apologize,
contrite and unconvincing as a haughty child.
I will not coax. My sister's efforts to cajole
her appetite go sour. Inside that head my mother's
younger selves already embrace dark, its earthy
welcome. When, outside, nurses rattle her IV pole,
A thousand mushrooms crowd to a keyhole.

Repeatedly the lights of this world beckon. For two days
after I arrive she eats. Her favourite nurse will rub her back.
She sleeps. The dreams! She maps her body with the sites
where pain alerts her to herself: her heel, her ankle, leg–the left
on Wednesday, right the day before–her stomach, and the
hand in which the needle's taped. The tournament
of pain and pleasure's almost done. She takes account
and calls us into her distress: Her daughters
will come with her into death. She'll brook no argument.
This is the one star in their firmament

because it's hers, the star that eats the dark which is
the life that scared her. Of course this is not spoken, that body
is not mine. Not mine that cavern of a mouth. When I arrive
I'm whole but, slowly, I repeat her words, her gesture animates
my jaw. It's cruel. Late in the day I lie down on the grass
and cry behind my sunglasses. At Braveheart's Bar

I drink a pint of beer. Trees move a little in the wind: nowhere
they need to go. I'm grateful too for the pigeon that seams a sky
as cloudless now as love's conceived to be. It drives a door ajar
Or frames a star within a star.

She does not want our deaths. She does not
even want her life. She opens her eyes to my sister
and closes them fast. She wants the blanket gone,
the sheet removed. With every exhalation she confirms
what she is willing to give up: her bed, her painted nails,
the look of someone well-fed, a woman to admire.
Her daughters—even they won't serve. Dismissed, they drive,
the morning of her death, southeast, to see the butterflies
which hatch and flutter on this country's border, hearts on fire.
What should they do there but desire?

Wind Like Prairie Wind

Cottonwoods ache in it.
Dense stands of Douglas fir
yawn faintly. Sheep

take shelter, crocuses retreat
into the earth. The caps
lift off the hives. This

is what happens *au fin
de siècle*, end of the year
of the monkey. Monkey

brain monkey-swings all those
branches on which we bang
our heads: Ah,

what we could be by
letting go!
Today I pry a platter of ice

from the pond and fling it—*smash*—
against the fencepost. Sky
clings to its brightness.

Not long, not nearly long
enough: *Anthem for the New
Nations*, inside, twisted loud. But

today I gather eggs, a hatful,
the first from the black ducks.
Those dark whole notes

roll, fruit from flowers, water
from Mountain Lesotho. Dollar Brand
in gold silk tunic, long

brown hands. The alder
are full of themselves, can't hold
themselves in, are waving their spirits

about. The day of ten eggs.
Mid-February. Thirteen years since
three friends met, and we took turns

paddling the *African Queen*, restored,
on Portage Inlet among swans, and Harry,
marvelling at all the blooming daffodils,

said he was going to move here soon.
This year unfolds
a wilder day, a keener

sun: no less
brilliant or searing or ready
to promise anything.

Clear to me now

what I planted this morning
was not cabbages but faith
in the future, little tag end
to I-know-not-what. In that

the exhilaration, giddy
as license to desire. I've
put my hand in next year,
thrown my lot in with earth's,
harrowed, sweated, given over

and stood back. Counted. Enough
kale for us, the neighbours,
ducks. Come spring, more
yellow promises: bunched blossoms.

See where the mind goes? Between
the lovely knots, a silk always
strong enough to bear its weight.
That throwing's what I love, what
I would give my life to.

Lacinato. Champion. *Rougette.*
Red cabbages dense and beautiful
as turbans, roses, words, like a row
of toothy kisses, sweet, unmanageable, raw.

The Mysteries

1

The balsam grove inhales dawn light
and wears it like a curtain by Vermeer.

Eastward the valley pockets mist. Cat tracks
burn the frosted stair, and someone else's

chickens have come here, come home,
to roost: a trio. Rod the Impaler,

Shelly the docile, Lolita, feisty,
feathered ship to the New World. She will

outlive us all, or die untouched,
unmatched, as Beth in *Little Women*.

I pull on my linen sweater, heavy
as our dog's long ears. I button jeans

and lean to kiss my sleeping husband.
A languorous warmth now to the haze, hair

flattened on the side on which he dreams.
The muscled tang between his lips

could raise new bread. Not merely tongue
but teeth. And thighs. How can I not

comply? It's spring: the greening
willow, hornbeam, rooted, sheltering

pleasures. And bulbs: the sharp, sedate,
the long-stemmed allium, the blues

that rise untended. His orgasm not clean-
edged or traceable, but a long crest

of colour in my ear and his full weight
brought to my back. A helicopter skims

the coral reefs off the Australian coast:
Who says when the tide turns?

2

I miss my ferry, catch the next.

3

The ship reverses, windows shudder, surge
past evergreens, arbutus, sailboats,

sky. The cliffs of the far islands blanch
and vanish. We nose into white light.

I think that this may happen when we die.
We will spin, simple, on some axis, burn

into white light, and then attend
inside, the troubled core: a strand

of something, maybe DNA, which augers
from the earth's core through the instep, up

the spine, the skull, and hooks us
to the nearest star. This holds us

upright. Outer space is not
the frigid night of sixties movies,

but teems with the unformed,
the not-yet. Caught between

worlds or between visions of the larger
world, we twist in open water,

trying to lose the dock, on all sides
rock, unreadable, half-treed. While at our feet

on the washroom stall's green tile, glitter,
like ash, strewn pink and blue and silver.

Some angel dematerialized. Bright fish,
the one that got away. Or child,

who shed the cells when pulling down
her jeans, rough on the living skin.

Heart Trail

At this curve in the path the rain

is like nothing except rain
sieved fine as chaff and let fall—
for what it is worth—wherever
it lands. My face turns up.

Invisible in the milky sky, frail
as shaved ice on green cedar. Still,

the locals call it rain. In the distance,
two hammers, eerie hoots
of children out of school on a Friday

before the end of April. Spangled.
Sawdust of bucked light. Scaled trout.

Encompassed by the bewildered
dog, who, roaming, bored, points
eight times out,

my feet encounter rock and root,
my face upturns: transfixed, my head's

the bright heart of a star.

The Same Words Over and Over

And in that quiet—
wildness. Can you hear the invitations?
The world is kissing you,
brushing against you.

— Carole Glasser Langille, "Winter"

I turned Carole's new poems face down
and, feeding the stove another wedge of fir,
curled into the blue back of the couch, meaning

to lie long enough to remember
lying beneath you. Instead I slept,
a light, blank sleep, and woke

with the same desire like a message
still in my fist. Now sun rows through
fast-moving cumulus, the sky looks

like the second coming. That night I wanted
everything you'd bring me, I missed nothing
that spilled from your beautiful mouth.

The neighbour's goose has freed herself
again and grazes in our field. Soon, past
comprehension, dark. No other lying like it. That night

I was sensitive as a sail: "ear
that listens to the wind," as empty of myself,
as full of starlight. Where has that sail

blown to now with your secrets? All of me
billowed beneath you, the heaviest
paper, watermarked, etched with your telling.

What did you tell? You rapped on my breastbone
with knuckles. Dark cracked in me, opened
a chasm, where who you were then

lives now. I would rather house you.
This void is voiceless and says
the same words over and over.

When you spoke, it rasped
untranslated from your belly through
your beautiful throat. I can't

repeat it: hunger, minutely described
and roving, the size of your mouth.
Chains of starlight ignited in sequence,

spiralled the shell of my ear.
It was clear you would never give
more. But that's my story. Yours was rough,

like your voice and the way you kept
hauling me in to you, how you aligned the words
'fucking' and 'angel,' the way you invited

proposals that would not rest in the same room
of your skull, let them in, let them
writhe and wrestle themselves out.

I kept a fire in the stove all afternoon. Thump
on my chest, an echo, improvise a new logic.
Tell me again where your mouth imagines itself.

Beet

That which has scavenged
pulverized rock to yield

an account of ourselves:
churlish, bloody-minded, sweet

beyond reason. Root
of the salt shore, size

of our fists or our hearts,
rimed, the prelingual

gift. More meat than
root, it knows its place

to be the middle of the plate
and brooks no argument:

compromise is not
in its vocabulary.

Honest. As the day is.
Long. Tailed. Leathered,

barked, or haired, and inside
luminous as pearl, as semen.

Turtle, shelled. It *is*
its home. It smells

unquestionable. Stark.
A root with teeth, not

genial not tame; it
will not marry us.

Almost, perhaps not in its
range of hearing. Its congress

is with lava, riprap, scat.
A fallen planet, we bear it

glazed in winter on white
china, and spear it with

a three-tined silver fork.

Migration

I'm driving through wet intersections at night
while traffic lights flash amber. *In love
with another, in love, in love* I'm driving away

from the house of a friend, having eaten soup
with her daughter, her mother, ornamented
the opulent spruce, held in my palm

for the length of *O Holy Night* the bird I
bought for her daughter's first Christmas, blown-glass,
copper-bright, with an ashy-feathered tail.

When I go back to my husband on Thursday we
will cut the young fir that sprang up
beneath the six-hundred-year-old yew

and drag it wet into the house, haul out
the mandarin box of glittering bells and Polish
paper stars, the chains of leathered cranberries

his sister strung. Years here of largesse. When
did we both stop counting? I drive home in the rain
the week before solstice under a waxing

moon, largest visible in more
than a century, closest to us, nearest to
the sun, knowing nothing for certain

except things refuse to remain
what they are. The treetop this year
may never get its star.

What the Brain Tells the Body
When He Enters the Room

I give over. I give up. You want the world.
Leave me out. Forget the way home. You want

the world on your tongue. Don't look
at your watch. Open your mouth, which believes

it will never be night. The second hand indicates
nothing; it signals the rift between wanting

and having. Ask. Ask again. Little
ragged flower, bud-nipped, triumphant.

Have I said, Among weeds? Have I said, Yellow?
What do I know of this except what

over the edge is? Open your legs. Lose
even the meaning of home. Soon.

Or you will be sick with cigarettes, caffeine
and longing. Already you're undone, and proud of it.

In the Spring of No Letters

Do I think of you often, my husband wants to know.
I lie and say no or lie and say yes.
I do not think of you, exactly.
My body has words with your ghost sometimes.

I lie and say no, or lie and say yes.
We are never upright when the truth is spoken.
My body has words with your ghost sometimes.
We speak in tongues, a lingual exchange.

We are never upright when the truth is spoken.
I am used up by what the body cannot parse.
We speak in tongues, a lingual exchange
I understand and do not at the same time.

I am used up by what the body cannot parse.
The sauna stove next door's alight again.
I understand this and do not at the same time.
Is time the issue? How many times, he asks.

Next door the sauna stove's alight again.
I know, for instance, from the smoke that it is evening.
Is time the issue? How many times he asks,
as if day were a pie: proportional, divisible, dessert.

For instance, from the smoke, I know it's evening,
I'm baking yams. The dog's content.
And day's a pie: proportional, divisible, dessert.
The smoke rises like a finer form of blossom.

I'm baking yams. The dog's content.
I do not think of you exactly.
The smoke rises like a finer form of blossom.
Do I think of you? My husband wants to know.

Breath of the Others

When a print's blown up
past knowledge of itself, we are
larger and softer-edged than life.

In a room filled with friends,
all packed close, we read,
each to ourselves but attuned

to the breath of the others.
This happens in daylight, the light
of late morning, with so much ahead

to move into. I read *Songs to Survive
the Summer*; it murmurs for years
with such tenderness. The sun

travels, the light drags its fingers
through coffee table dust, till
someone gets hungry and goes

to the kitchen for pretzels,
returning to pass the bag round. A slow
order to this: the earth's tongue

in its cheek. Glazed in the light
and salted by the sprawl, the pages turn
or fold. Heads rest in laps,

on shoulders. In the quiet between decades
we are eloquent, unmade:
our feet in the hands of friends.

How to Be Happy

When my husband came home he gave me
a little pamphlet, a folded paper

an old man had pressed into his hand in town.
E Bahsler had it printed: *How To*

Be Happy, a grainy rose ghosting the title, his
phone number at the end. Inside he told

of Joseph Scriven, who, a century before,
survived the drowning of his almost-bride

and turned from suicide to write
What a Friend We Have in Jesus.

About himself, E Bahsler says:
"I am now an old man, I am 85 years old.

When I was young I was a big sinner,
I drank, I smoked, I went to dances,

played my accordion at dances, I also
became miserable and not happy."

Beside Ourselves

A kind of love will take the air
in rhythm with the limbs, the walk in spring
from Sarah's house to

campus grounds, alive
with ducks and rabbits.
When you turn your gaze upon it—

not much there. Used
condoms, two discarded notes.
No less heartfelt for that, no less

distressed. English ivy
dragging down or holding up
the Garry oak. The one

I almost ran the stop sign
staring at, its wiry reach
into this year's blue. So here's

the puzzle: at what point
does heartwood, knuckled
bark, become

those liquid fingertips
the sky suckles?
Which feed, themselves, on sky.

I'm sorry, friends, herewith apologies
for this spring scene. For the robin
—you, snowbound, you especially

must believe—who then ferries

another crumb of duff
to her elegant nest wedged impossibly

over the office door. So we
can no longer exit into Oregon grape.
So the fluorescent hum's replaced

by earthy rustle, overhead. So suddenly
what we thought upheld us
now starts to build new sky. You see,

it doesn't stop, does not stop
                                    ever. Even
when she settles—that expectant arc
to back, to beak—she's listening,

her whole body newly Ear.

Strawberry Fields

When the plane sounds overhead
the strawberry pickers stop their work—

this is the point: first their union
with the red centres, then the wavelike

rising to the roar of another
wing. An engine, this or that, is not

the point. Small fragrant heart-sacs
of juice. The lumbering gunmetal span that

mimics the muscle of thought. We're twinned
with dirt, with steel: these are

the limits of our being, and only
in a field like this, sunlit,

with others like us dreaming
"whipped cream soon, preserves later,"

knees in the dirt, and the shuddering
arc of the inconceivable pulling us up,

only in that moment are we
balanced: at the pivot, heads up, rooted,

our fingers dripping juice. Then we are set in our ways.
Gripped. Gems. Perfectly transmitting light.

Mid-March, Pender Island

At winter's end we haul debris,
the lichen-crippled
alder, fallen birch. I drag the brush,
you set the sticks against themselves.

Above us, round the valley, trees are animal
in wind. They own it. They own
every hope that we had once and then
outgrew. The breeze becomes them.

I leave you to poke the fire.

Here's fuel: discarded Christmas wrapping,
here's the string. The wooden
ornamental dwarf that's lost its shine.
Here: all the labels, me to you
and back again. And now

the pine. Parched to its oils
and brittle as old wire, its needles spur things
on. The frost retreats; we're haloed
by wet lawn. I leave you standing then,

head east with the machete, pause
to eye the walnut, the sapped plum. This month

or next, again, they will insinuate
their pointed appetites
into the world. Enough: I want to
feed the ruthless blaze their stupid
hearts.
            We are, we are not
winged and faithless.

Between us in the hedge's deeper gloom
a dozen geese glow like white stones.

The sinuous trunk of the weeping
birch, the sky-riddled stream
of the lane's dark—and what
the two engender is the same.

                    I reach

for a caught vine, dead to the touch—
corps-à-corps: a tussle
hand to hand. I worry it. Put down
the blade, the rake, my gloves

and reach again.

                    Daily the new shoots
rise up, curious, steady.

The Fever Breaks

Morning lies on the couch
a little heartsick, afraid,
a little on the edge

of nausea. She looks up at
her husband's dark
leather jacket hanging

on the coat tree
by its cunning neck loop
and what she sees is

the ripped fabric of the world.
This is not metaphor.
The world itself. Tattered,

worn right through and
flapping. She can't know
what, if anything, is

on the other side. It will take her
whole life to learn
about loneliness:

how she has avoided it,
how it has always been there,
companionable, constant, home.

Hunting

Peace is the name of the river
you set your traps along,

the rose you will plant,
postwar, in our yard.

Give me something sharper, with an edge.
What I wield is blunt and will not

break the skin. It's imprecise.
I use my hands. I feel

as well as hear the crack
of dislocated bone, of tendons

wrenched. The doe's eyes:
wells of understanding, foggy

telescopic pits. She surely
cannot lift her head again;

her look will kill me. I'm kneeling
on a rocky slope with someone

at my back, and it's for him, for his
approval I've gone hunting. I bend

to the task, begin to take
the animal apart. What I cannot bear

is this separate place, here
in a being who watches horrified

what her hands unfold. I snap
the shoulder. Down but not dead.

There is no way to say this prettily.
She lifts her head.

Give me what's mine, I wailed or wished.
Give me what binds us: fury

that we can neither devour nor
integrate the world.
World of the flesh,

you said in your sixties. A testing ground,
penance, until we gather at the river ready

to shed the trappings of this life.
High light, no sun, no shadows.

By then you'd done your penance, Dad, worked
to old age, ill health, raised a second family

for a wife embittered at what you
would not give her, at what you'd poured

into the woman in the snapshot
handed me, oh, years past that:

your first wife. Who could handle
no more cool headedly than you

your rages or her own, the north, its poverty,
breathtaking glossy pelts extracted

from your trapline in the snow. She took
your son to the house of another man.

And after that you gave up dancehalls, drink,
fixed your eyes on the quiet highway, curbed

what scarred your knuckles and your
heart. Grande Prairie under snow. Peace

is the name of the river you had set your traps along,
the rose you planted, postwar, in our yard.

Here's where I begin to know you. The bush
blooms domesticated sunsets in your hands,

a decade of them, more, each petal
a perfect thumbnail huge as your own,

whose cuticles are black with oil by then.
The engines of the city deafen

till you no longer hear your daughters'
high-pitched discontent or their

angry mother's jibes. You stop attending
the Baptist services that terrify my sister,

that I love: full-throated hymns, preacher
who will not stay where we would have him,

unruly congregation, alive to God's word
the way that glass or wood's alive

to what it's sung. Some speak in tongues, and I
don't know where this is going. I missed

you, Dad, how you would give me
that long gaze of love one time and not

another, suddenly remote in the blinding
arctic landscape with your gun and knife.

Some spoke in tongues. You gave me
something sharper, with an edge.

Do you recall the time
when, at wit's end, I kicked your shin

repeatedly? It worked; you turned on me
the look I longed for, look that burned;

you picked me up; you shook me,
shouted. Threw me across the room. I

snapped the shoulder. Began to take the animal
apart. At this time or another I helped

you pluck a pheasant's radiant feathers
for my mother's hat. This is long before

you label me a slut before my sisters: imprecise.
I learn your habit of forgetting too

and forget much. There's little left of you.
My younger sister has your fine dark eyes.

I've nothing but your hands in miniature,
shapely, graceful, wanting to be up against

whatever moves, is geared or petalled
and unfolds in the heat. Adoration

of this life's the gravest sin, and we're both
guilty. But say it's Sunday morning. Say you've

touched your fingers to my head. The hymns
are rising through my skull. And now

your huge and lovely hand uproots
a pencil from your jacket, turns

the church program inside out,
and on its blank side draws me

images of animals on snow:
wolf and beaver, wildcat and doe.

Perfect Seam

The long tail of my history
no longer represents me.
                —Chase Twichell, "Imaginary Dokusan: Barking Dog"

The dog that lies on my bed while I write
surrenders in sleep to his world, body

a docile comma, hips and tail curving under
as they must have when he spilled

with his seven brothers and sisters onto grass.
His coat is not long or thick enough to ward off wind or rain,

its function a copper beauty that calls hands to it, to how
the grain of it collides on the back of the thighs

like the perfect seam of a woman's stocking.
A muzzle soft as heavy velvet, silvered.

What does he teach you? To give yourself up
to what wants you, over and over, riding with ease

on those superbly calloused paws. Look
at the ligament connecting foot and hip!

How his coat shifts from gold to cedar in the shade.
And between the whorls on his rump the delicate fold

that housed what might have been desire,
beautiful now and empty What we call heart

in dogs is steady imposition of their will upon
what thwarts them: stormy water. A deceptive

grouse. The human heart. How he burns
his place in that landscape thoughtlessly, without

intent, ribcage heaving the newly sniffed-out
dream. Around him the world rebuilding itself.

Notes on the poems

The title "The tiny silver luck of minnows" is a phrase borrowed from a Jane Hirschfield poem called "The Wedding" in her collection *The October Palace* (HarperCollins, 1994).

"*Kouros*," literally "youth," is the term for a form of Greek statuary common from 700-500 BC. Massive, often larger than lifesized and usually stone, the *kouros* was a standing, frontally presented male nude, emblematic of the heroic and of the generative power of perpetual youth. Serving both as votive offerings and grave markers, *kouroi* embodied the ideal of excellence, a fusion of the beautiful and the good.

The phrase quoted in "The Same Words Over and Over" is borrowed from Carole Glasser Langille's poem "Corresponding," which appears with "Winter" in her collection *In Cannon Cave* (Brick Books, 1997).

"Strawberry Fields" is a response to John Terpstra's "Small Voices" (from *Devil's Punch Bowl*, The St. Thomas Poetry Series, 1998); the quoted line is from that poem.

Acknowledgements

I'm grateful to the Canada Council for its support during the writing of these poems.

Many have appeared in the following publications: *Event*, *Fiddlehead*, *The Peralta Press*, *Prairie Fire*, *New Canadian Poetry* (Fitzhenry & Whiteside), *Vintage 99: League of Canadian Poets Anthology* (Ronsdale Press), and *Intersections* (Banff Centre Press). Thank you to all of the editors. "Outdoor Baptism" was awarded the Robinson Jeffers Tor House Prize in 2000 and published in *The Tor House Newsletter*. "Nice Girls" was part of the BC Poetry in Transit project.

These poems received much valuable input from participants and faculty of the 1999 Banff Writers' Studio. My thanks to everyone there for inspiration and good company, and especially to Don McKay, lavish with his library, his wit, and his remarkable eye and ear.

I was introduced to British artist Sophie Ryder's immense bronze "Dancing Hares" at her Life Force exhibition in Bath in 1999 and have been an avid follower of her work since. I'm grateful for her generosity in allowing "Blue Hare" to grace the cover of *Shameless*.

Marlene Cookshaw is the author of three previous collections of poetry, most recently *Double Somersaults* (Brick Books, 1999). Born in Lethbridge, Alberta, she has lived more than twenty years on the west coast of BC, part of that time on Pender Island, where she keeps a large garden. In Victoria she edits *The Malahat Review*.